Robert E. Lee

Commander of the Confederate Army

Alison Gaines

Cavendish
Square

New York

Published in 2019 by Cavendish Square Publishing, LLC
243 5th Avenue, Suite 136, New York, NY 10016

Library of Congress Cataloging-in-Publication Data

Names: Gaines, Alison, author.
Title: Robert E. Lee : Commander of the Confederate Army / Alison Gaines.
Description: First edition. | New York : Cavendish Square, 2018. | Series:
Hero or Villain?: Claims and Counterclaims | Includes bibliographical
references and index. | Audience: Grade: 7 to 12.
Identifiers: LCCN 2017058834 (print) | LCCN 2017059321 (ebook) |
ISBN 9781502635303 (e-Book) | ISBN 9781502635297 (library bound : alk. paper) |
ISBN 9781502635310 (pbk. : alk. paper)
Subjects: LCSH: Lee, Robert E. (Robert Edward), 1807-1870. |
Generals--Confederate States of America--Biography. | United
States--History--Civil War, 1861-1865--Biography. | Confederate States of America. Army--Biography.
Classification: LCC E467.1.L4 (ebook) | LCC E467.1.L4 G189 2018 (print) |
DDC 973.7/3092 [B] --dc23
LC record available at https://lccn.loc.gov/2017058834

Editorial Director: David McNamara
Editor: Michael Spitz
Copy Editor: Rebecca Rohan
Associate Art Director: Amy Greenan
Designer: Amy Greenan/Christina Shults
Production Coordinator: Karol Szymczuk
Photo Research: J8 Media

The photographs in this book are used by permission and through the courtesy of:
Photo credits: Cover Stocktrek Images, Inc./Alamy Stock Photo; p.4 Hulton Archive/Getty Images; p. 5 (used throughout the book) Wikimedia Commons/File:Cantino planisphere (1502).jpg/Public Domain; p. 7 David Lyons/Alamy Stock Photo; p. 8 Internet Archive Book Images/Wikimedia Commons/File:Popular life of Gen. Robert Edward Lee (1874) (14786627683).jpg; p. 11, 15, 21 Buyenlarge/Getty Images; p. 12, 74 Library of Congress; p. 16 Chronicle/Alamy Stock Photo; p. 26-27, 90 Stock Montage/Getty Images; p. 30, 59, 60 Universal History Archive/Getty Images; p. 36 Kean Collection/Archive Photos/Getty Images; p. 37 Júlio Reis/Wikimedia Commons/File:US Secession map 1861.svg/CC BY SA 3.0; p. 39, 70 North Wind Picture Archives; p. 40 Bettmann/Getty Images; p. 46 Andrew Joseph Russell/Gilder Lehrman Collection/Bridgeman Images; p. 48 Christian F. Schwerdt/Chicago History Museum/Bridgeman Images; p. 57 MPI/Getty Images; p. 58 Photo12/UIG/Getty Images; p. 62 Popperfoto/Getty Images; p. 67 William Edward West/Wikimedia Commons/File:Robert E Lee 1838.jpg/Public Domain; 72 Mark Harris/Photodisc/Getty Images; p. 85 Konstantinks/Shutterstock.com; p. 94 Gado Images/Alamy Stock Photo; p. 90 Carol Highsmith/Library of Congress/Wikimedia Commons/File:Lee Chapel.jpg/Public Domain.

Printed in the United States of America

CON TENTS

A portrait of Robert E.
Lee, circa 1845

The Virginian

Robert E. Lee commanded the Army of Northern Virginia and, eventually, the whole Confederate Army during the American Civil War. His name conjures up wildly different associations in the minds of different Americans. As with many historical figures, people learn about Lee culturally, and the facts are filtered through public opinion. In order to provide a more holistic view of Lee, it's important to explore the roots of the controversy and the context of nineteenth century America. Beyond our own personal differences and biases, who was he, and what can we learn?

By the end of the Civil War, Lee was the face of the Confederate Army and its general-in-chief. This is how he lives in cultural memory today. For most of the war, he only commanded part of the army, the

Army of Northern Virginia. He had a long career before the Civil War as well, all of it spent as a commissioned officer in the US Army, and most of it spent doing engineering work, not combat. Lee was fifty-four years old by the time the Civil War began. His was not a life spent crusading for Southern values, the Confederacy, or any of the other popular phrases associated with the war. It was mostly a life spent doing what he was told, and what he believed he *should* do. Before diving into the man's inner thoughts and the country's struggles, here is a brief overview of his career.

Family and Early Career

Lee was born into a family whose men staunchly identified themselves with being soldiers and with their home state of Virginia. The shadow of George Washington also followed him from a young age. His father, Henry "Light Horse Harry" Lee, had served in the Revolutionary War under Washington. Robert was the fifth child born to Anne and Harry. He did not grow up particularly wealthy because Harry, while he had been an asset to the Revolutionary cause, had taken a downhill turn later in life and gotten himself into a lot of debt.

Lee attended the United States Military Academy at West Point for college and graduated in 1829. Upon graduation, he was offered a commission with the Corps of Engineers. His first appointment took him to Cockspur Island, Georgia, where he supervised the building of a fort. In 1831, Lee married a distant cousin and childhood friend, Mary Randolph Custis. For the next fifteen years, Lee went wherever he was told on various engineering jobs. He

Stratford Hall, where Lee was born and lived the first few years of his life

STRATFORD, BIRTH PLACE OF ROBERT E. LEE.

A depiction of Lee's childhood home

supervised more fort construction, worked as an assistant to the chief of engineers in Washington, traveled to the Great Lakes region to help settle a border disagreement between Ohio and Michigan, worked for three years on waterfront improvement on the Mississippi River, and lived in Fort Hamilton, New York, working on harbor fortifications. During this time, in which he was promoted to the rank of captain, he was often away from his growing family. Mary had given birth to their sixth child by 1846, when the war with Mexico began.

The war with Mexico was Lee's first exposure to combat. He did some engineering work as well as some combat, reconnoitering on horseback for Major General Winfield Scott. Scott was quite impressed with Lee as a soldier and invited him into his inner circle, or "little cabinet," of four advisors.

After the war ended in 1848, Lee was assigned more engineering work, this time at Fort Carroll in Baltimore. Three years later, he took a different professional direction and became superintendent of his alma mater, West Point Academy, where his eldest son was currently in attendance. In 1855, though, he received another military assignment that brought him to Texas. Unlike his other posts, this one involved combat command, not engineering, as he commanded two squadrons whose duties included protecting settlers from Native Americans.

The Decision

Soon after, the Confederacy formed, and a civil war was on the horizon. After the Confederacy was officially organized in February 1861, Lee received job offers from both the Union and the Confederate armies. He did not decide on either right away. In letters, he expressed that he did not think this war was a good idea, but that if it came to it, he would defend his home state. Virginia's secession on April 17 sealed the deal for Lee. "I hope I may never be called upon to draw my sword," Lee wrote in a letter to his sister after telling the Union Army that he would not be joining them.

Lee began the war in Richmond as an advisor to Jefferson Davis, the president of the Confederacy. In May 1862, however, he was asked to fill in for a wounded colleague, Joseph Eggleston Johnston, and his Army of Northern Virginia. Originally, Lee only expected to stay until Johnston recovered, but he ended up staying with this army for the duration of the war.

Lee's early battles earned him the nickname "Granny Lee," for his timidity and hesitancy to make bold moves. His reputation improved with victories in the Seven Days' Battles and at the Battle of Second Manassas (also known as the Second Battle of Bull Run). One of Lee's major strategies was the Maryland campaign. In September 1862, he made the decision to take his army north to take attention away from Virginia, disrupt the east/west railway line, and perhaps gain support from Confederate-leaning citizens in Maryland. He moved fifty-five thousand troops into Maryland. It was here that the Battle of Sharpsburg (Antietam) was fought, the bloodiest single day of the war and a Confederate loss.

The following year, Lee decided to go north again, this time to Pennsylvania. His goal was to keep attention away from Virginia and to stay on the offensive. Lee learned that the Union army was concentrating at Gettysburg, and this led to the other famous battle and major Confederate loss of the war.

In May 1864, Ulysses S. Grant was put in charge of the whole Union army, and Lee's objective became to keep Grant away from Richmond, the Confederacy's capital, at all costs. The war dragged on for nearly another year before the Union finally took control of the Southside Railroad, and Richmond had to be evacuated. Lee's surrender to Grant came days later.

Post-War Lee

After the war, Lee received many job offers. The one he took was president of a small college in Lexington, Virginia. This was a somewhat familiar role for him, a gentler way to be

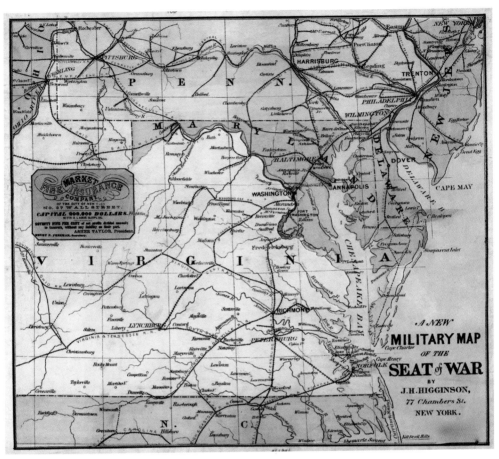

Before the Civil War, Virginia and what is now West Virginia were
one state.

Martha and George Washington. Although George died before Lee was born, George was a lifetime role model for Lee.

in command, and reminiscent of his time as superintendent at West Point. Washington College had a small student body, made up of only white men. He made a few policy changes there, including changing the curriculum. He added classes in postclassical literature, law, journalism, and modern languages. He also got rid of the rule that required students to attend chapel every day, although he himself attended often. He lived in a house provided by the college with his whole family.

Lee died on October 12, 1870. After this, Washington College was renamed to Washington and Lee University. Lee would likely have been highly honored to be united in name and legacy with his idol, George Washington. When he died, his wife and three of his children surrounded him.

The Army of Northern Virginia

Lee assumed command of the Army of Northern Virginia in May 1862. Previously, it had gone under a few different names, including the Department of Alexandria and the Potomac Department. Previous commanders before Lee included P.G.T. Beauregard and Joseph E. Johnston. When Johnston assumed control in July 1861, he began calling his department the Army of the Potomac. (The Potomac River runs between Virginia and Maryland.) Confusingly, the Army of the Potomac is also what the rival Union department called itself.

When Lee became the commander, he unofficially named his group the Army of Northern Virginia. Unlike the Union's Army of the Potomac, the Army of Northern Virginia had steady command for several years. Lee served as its commander from May 1862 until shortly before the end of the war, when Davis appointed him General-in-Chief. Over the course of the war, the Union Army of the Potomac had six commanders: Irvin McDowell, George B. McClellan, Ambrose E. Burnside, Joseph Hooker, George Gordon Meade, and John Parke.

Lee did his best to keep morale high among his men. He encouraged them to be a Christian army and

Soldiers of the 4th New York Heavy Artillery pose with a siege gun in Arlington, Virginia, in 1863.

admonished them not to engage in any looting or pillaging after some of the later battles. Using religion may have helped his soldiers feel more as if there were something to fight for, and some of them used it to feel morally superior to the Union men. Even so, the Confederacy had a huge problem with desertion, especially toward the end of the war, when many people had been drafted for the duration. It's estimated that a couple months before the end of the war, two-thirds of the Confederate army was missing. The Army of Northern Virginia's battle flag is the flag most associated with the Confederacy today.

Robert E. Lee as a
young soldier

Lee in Context

By Lee's time, the United States was still a very young country. Lee's birth came only thirty-one years after the signing of the Declaration of Independence. Even by the time of the Civil War, the country had not yet celebrated its one-hundredth birthday. Lee's father, Harry, had fought during the Revolution and played a role in the country's early political development. The country's founding and recent break from British rule was still fresh in national memory. Many of the causes of the Civil War point back to the "peculiar institution" of slavery.

Divergence of North and South

The North provides an interesting contrast to the South and can help shed light on the South's treatment of slavery. During the early years of the country's development, colonies and individual counties made decisions to ban the slave trade.

The original framers of the Constitution weren't sure how to represent slaves. They came up with the "three-fifths compromise," which counted slaves as three-fifths of a person in terms of representation. Native Americans were not represented at all. Part of this compromise was that the slave trade would be allowed to continue until 1808. That original Constitution also contained fugitive slave laws, allowing slaves who escaped to free states to be returned to their owners. Some southern states continued to engage in the slave trade into the 1800s.

Banning the slave trade did not equal banning slavery itself. In most cases, states tackled the issue of the transatlantic slave trade before the issue of slavery. Vermont became the first state to outlaw slavery outright in 1777. In that same year, North Carolina took a turn in the other direction and outlawed private manumissions, or the ability of individual slave owners to free their slaves. Some states began to pass laws allowing gradual emancipation and private manumission, but fugitive slave laws often led to the wrongful arrest of free blacks, especially if they did not have their freedom papers on them.

The Northeast, despite having outlawed slavery on a state-by-state basis long before the Civil War began, was not full of abolitionists. The Northern economy had begun to rely more on manufacturing and industry than on agriculture. The same could not be said for the South, which relied heavily on the agrarian economy and, therefore, on slavery. While the wealthy people in the South were those who owned plantations and many slaves, wealthy people in the North were those who owned mills and factories, largely operated by poorer whites and the immigrant workforce. Many of those places made textiles, and the industry of the North relied on the cotton economy of the South.

Many Northern businessmen needed to maintain a relationship with their "Southern brethren." While abolitionists opposed slavery on moral grounds, Northern industrialists opposed it on economic ones. The Northern industrialists subscribed to the Republican values of an "expanding, enterprising, and competitive society," as historian Eric Foner put it. Allowing slavery to expand into the new parts of the country went against these beliefs. Slavery kept the power in the hands of the few elites who were born into plantation families. Northerners liked the idea, however theoretical, that anyone could achieve upward mobility. The industrial economy was more conducive to this.

New Territories and Popular Sovereignty

As the country grew and added states, the question always arose of whether the new states would be free or slave states. States began as territories, and the United States had several territories turning into states in the years leading up to the war. The Northwest Territory, for instance, was mostly made of land ceded by the original colony of Virginia after the Revolutionary War. It comprised the land south of the Great Lakes, west of the Appalachians, and east of the Mississippi River. The Northwest Ordinance, set in motion by a committee headed by Thomas Jefferson, laid out the road map for how future territories would turn into states. When the population reached sixty thousand free inhabitants, they could send a draft of their constitution to the US Congress. Congress would admit it as a state, provided that the constitution outlined a Republican government.

The ordinance allowed no fewer than three and no more than five states to be made out of the territory. It allowed basic rights to citizens living in the territories, such as freedom of religion and the right to a trial by jury. The sixth article of the ordinance is what it is most known for: it banned slavery and involuntary servitude from the territories. It only banned slavery going forward and did not affect the already established slaves and slave owners there. Ohio was the first state to join the Union from the territories in 1803. Indiana, Illinois, Michigan, and Wisconsin followed.

The next big acquisition, the largest land acquisition in the country's history, was the Louisiana Purchase in 1803. The land purchased extended from west Florida in the south to Montana in the north, and went as far west as the Rocky Mountains. This area had been owned by the French. Napoleon was eager to sell, and the United States was eager to buy. The United States paid the French $15 million (about $313 million in modern day currency). Of course, this again opened up the question of the future of

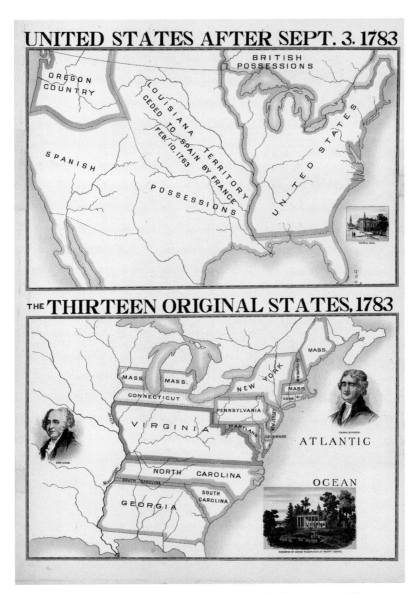

The original thirteen colonies are shown in the lower map. The Northwest Territory (the modern-day Midwest) was originally part of Virginia, Massachusetts, and Connecticut.

slavery and whether it would be allowed in the new territory. This question was answered with the next piece of legislation, the Maine-Missouri Compromise.

In 1818, Missouri, part of the Louisiana Territory, wanted to become a state. Congress decided to admit both Missouri and Maine (which was also up for statehood) as slave and free states, respectively, to keep the balance equal. Attached to this compromise was the provision that slavery would then be prohibited in the Louisiana Territory, north of Missouri. In 1854, yet another piece of legislation would overturn this.

Stephen Douglas, the chair of the Senate Committee on Territories, championed the Kansas-Nebraska Act. He offered a bill that would leave the slavery decision up to the individual territories. This passed. The Missouri Compromise would have banned slavery from both Kansas and Nebraska, but Douglas's bill included an amendment repealing the compromise. Slavery was now left up to popular sovereignty. A new political party, the Republican Party, was formed in opposition to the Kansas-Nebraska Act and popular sovereignty. The Republican Party wanted to disallow slavery entirely.

The introduction of popular sovereignty precipitated "Bleeding Kansas." Thanks to popular sovereignty, the area of Kansas was open to migrations of pro- and anti-slavery individuals fighting a border war, which included John Brown's massacre at Pottawatomie in 1856. The fighting known as "Bleeding Kansas" began in 1854 and mostly ended in 1859, but it did continue through the Civil War.

The War With Mexico

The Mexican-American War, which transpired between 1846 and 1848, was another war fought over slavery. In the beginning of the nineteenth century, Mexico included all of what is today California, Texas, New Mexico, Utah, Nevada, Arizona, and parts of Colorado and Wyoming. In 1836, Texas broke away from Mexico with the help of the United States, which had hoped to secure the land (the Civil War was not the first time the "Lone Star Republic" seceded from its government). The United States added Texas as a state in 1846 but ran into disagreements with Mexico on where the border with Mexico would be. President Polk was willing to go to war for this land and moved on this decision when Mexico refused to sell some of its territory to the United States. When Congress declared war, it was with a few opposition votes. The congressmen voting "nay" believed that the new territory would be turned into slave states, and they weren't wrong. Later on, popular sovereignty would be declared.

The culmination of the war happened when General Winfield Scott's army, of which Robert E. Lee was a part, moved on Mexico City. Mexico surrendered early in 1848. The Treaty of Guadalupe Hidalgo secured half of Mexico's territory for the United States: the entire Southwest and California. The treaty also established the Rio Grande as the Texas-Mexico border. Finally, the United States paid Mexico $15 million, allowing it to be said that the land was bought, not seized, from Mexico.

The American Colonization Society

Some groups came up with "solutions" for slavery and its aftereffects, but some of these solutions were nearly as problematic or harmful as slavery itself. One such group was the American Colonization Society. Robert Finley, a white Presbyterian minister from New Jersey, had the idea that blacks should be sent to a colony elsewhere, preferably in Africa. Like some other whites who did not support slavery, he believed that blacks could never truly achieve equality with whites in the United States, because of the deep-seeded racism in the country. He also had religious motivations, believing that sending "civilized and Christianized" people to Africa would spread Christianity.

Finley's brother-in-law, Elias Caldwell, joined up with him and helped recruit others to the cause, including Francis Scott Key, who wrote the poem that became the national anthem. At a meeting in 1816, they gained support from Henry Clay, then the Speaker of the House. Clay, however, supported colonization for different reasons. He owned slaves himself, and the idea of transporting freed black people to another continent appealed to him. Where freed and enslaved blacks could communicate with each other, freed blacks could encourage slaves to rebel. Slave owners desperately wanted to discourage slave rebellions. The colonization society began to attract two strains of people: those who believed in colonization as a humanitarian solution, and those who believed it would help slavery continue to exist in the United States.

Some Northerners who did not support slavery were critical of the idea of colonization. William Lloyd Garrison started out as a colonization supporter, believing that slavery was an evil from which the nation had to gradually free itself. He saw colonization as a way to help those who had been freed. His views changed, and he started to believe that colonization was not humanitarian at all. It simply took people from their homes and deported them. He started a newsletter called the *Liberator*, which mostly had a black readership, in which he spoke out against his previous belief that slavery could be ended gradually or with moderation:

> I do not wish to think, or speak, or write, with moderation. No! No! Tell a man whose house is on fire, to give moderate alarm; tell him to moderately rescue his wife from the hands of the ravisher; tell the mother to gradually extricate her babe from the fire into which is has fallen; - but urge me not to use moderation in a cause like the present.

For Garrison, the problem of slavery was like a house on fire—the time for moderation and civility had passed.

"Servile Rebellions"

Slave owners lived in fear of slave revolts, which they tended to call "servile rebellions." The main rebellion that stoked this fear was Nat Turner's in 1831. Turner belonged to the Turner Plantation in Southampton, Virginia, and was born into a very spiritual family. Turner's master encouraged his slaves to attend worship with him and his family. He saw Nat as someone with promising intellect and encouraged

A deeply religious man, Nat Turner would preach to his fellow slaves.

him to read the Bible. Turner did this regularly. In doing so, he concluded that slavery went against God's teaching that all people have equal dignity, and he began to believe that he had a calling to correct this. He experienced visions and began to see himself as a messiah figure.

Turner did escape once, for about thirty days, but returned. For him, escape was not the solution. Abolishing slavery was, even if through violent means. His time came in August 1831. He had amassed eight followers, and they began at the house of Turner's current owner, John Travis. They murdered Travis, his wife, and his four children with axes. The group then moved to other farms and gathered about seventy more followers. They killed over fifty white people, about half of whom were women and children, in a twenty-mile radius.

Local whites reacted with increased violence. It's estimated that as many as two hundred black people were killed, and more were tortured. Turner himself escaped into the woods for about six weeks until a white man discovered him on October 30. He was tried and hanged on November 11.

In response, the South grew even more terrified of their slaves being able to rebel. Throughout the South, legislation was passed that further limited the rights of slaves and free blacks. There were new penalties for educating slaves. Slaves had even fewer rights in terms of their right to preach and gather for religious services.

John Brown at Harpers Ferry

William Lloyd Garrison was not representative of all Northern attitudes against slavery, but his giving such a radical and fiery voice to abolitionism caught the attention of the South. Another fierce abolitionist, John Brown, took even more extreme measures and captured the attention of the opposition shortly before the war began.

Brown, a white man, kept a station on the Underground Railroad in Richmond, Ohio. In 1855, he went with his four sons to Kansas to fight against the pro-slavery contingent in "Bleeding Kansas." He earned the nickname "Osawatomie" because he headed up an abolitionist colony in that Kansas town. The following year, he, two of his sons, and four others killed five pro-slavery men; this was the aforementioned Pottawatomie Massacre. Much like Nat Turner, Brown believed he was carrying out the will of God, murders notwithstanding.

In 1859, Brown carried out the raid for which he is famous. He envisioned a huge slave rebellion sweeping the South. He began his raid in Harpers Ferry, Virginia (what is now West Virginia). With twenty-one men following him and several hostages (both black and white), Brown captured the federal armory in Harpers Ferry. The group locked itself inside a firehouse. Maryland militiamen, many of them drunk and armed, started to take matters into their own hands and shot one of the raiders (an escaped slave) on sight. President Buchanan dispatched Lee (then a lieutenant

Like Nat Turner, John Brown made extreme attempts to disarm the slavery system, and he was hanged for it.

colonel) and Lee's former student at West Point, J.E.B. Stuart, to defuse the situation. When Lee arrived, the rowdy militia deferred to him. Lee wrote a letter asking Brown and the raiders to "peaceably surrender themselves and restore the pillaged property." He also noted that it would be impossible for Brown and his men to escape—Lee had the armory surrounded on all sides with Marines. Stuart walked over to the firehouse and handed the letter to the raiders.

Brown immediately tried to negotiate, but Lee and Stuart wouldn't hear of it. Lee signaled the Marines. They eventually broke through the doors using a ladder as a battering ram. They quickly captured Brown, and all the hostages were safe. Ten of Brown's men were killed in the gunfire, including two of his sons. Brown was tried and hanged in December of that year. Up to the end of his life, he believed he was doing God's will and seemed to exhibit no fear.

Brown had asked fellow abolitionists Harriet Tubman and Frederick Douglass to join him in the raid. Tubman was ill, and Douglass believed the mission would fail (he was right). Outspoken abolitionists like Brown and Garrison made slavery into a binary issue. This polarization of the issue of slavery is seen as one of the factors that tipped the scales toward war.

"John Brown's Body" became a popular anthem of the Union. Julia Ward Howe would later write her poem "The Battle Hymn of the Republic" using the same melody.

The First Republican President

When Abraham Lincoln ran for president in 1860, he was one of four candidates in the general election. The current president, James Buchanan, was at the head of a party that was splintering. The Democrats were split between those who supported slavery and those who didn't. The party established two separate tickets: Stephen Douglas, a Northerner who had run against Buchanan in 1856 (as well as campaigned against Lincoln in 1858 to represent Illinois in the US Senate), and John Cabell Breckinridge, Buchanan's vice president. Douglas would later support Lincoln's call for troops, and Breckinridge would go on to serve in the Confederate army after fleeing his native state of Kentucky. A third party, the Constitutional Union Party, also put forward a candidate, John Bell. The Constitutional Union Party was new as well, and it appealed to former Whigs and people in border states, like Virginia. Bell won Virginia, but interestingly, Robert E. Lee cast his vote for Breckinridge. The newly formed Republican Party did not struggle with the disunity that the Democrats did, as it had established itself in opposition to slavery.

Lincoln did not win a majority of the vote, but running against three candidates and a disjointed Democratic party, he did not have to. He achieved 40 percent of the popular vote and 180 of the 303 electoral votes. Nearly 70 percent of voters in the 1860 election did not want slavery to expand into the territories, and it was this issue upon which Lincoln based his platform.

With Lincoln's victory, the Republican Party gained control of the presidency and the House of Representatives, but Democrats kept control of the Senate. Southerners, especially those who supported slavery, felt that their country had been taken over by people who did not have their interests at heart. Seven states seceded shortly after the election: South Carolina, Mississippi, Florida, Alabama, Georgia, Louisiana, and Texas. President Buchanan did not do much to stop the illegal secessions.

Government by a Unified Class

The Confederate States of America officially formed itself in Montgomery, Alabama, in the spring of 1861. Seven states had already seceded from the Union, and several others would follow once the war officially started. Each state decided to secede on its own. A former South Carolina senator, Robert Barnwell Rhett, proposed that instead of each state fending for itself, the South should make a new national government.

When the Confederacy was born, it was mostly made of up members of the wealthy planter class. Several who took part in the Montgomery Convention had served in government previously. Among the delegates was Howell Cobb, former speaker of the US House of Representatives and treasury secretary for President Buchanan. Over a dozen of the delegates had previously served in the US House or Senate. All of these men were just one generation removed from the original Founding Fathers, who had framed the US Constitution.

The Confederate framers banded together in the first place because they felt that their way of life was under attack. Therefore, their new constitution had slavery as a priority. The right to own slaves was upheld, as was the right to transport slaves between states. The international slave trade was outlawed.

This was a document by slave owners and for slave owners. Regular Confederate citizens, it should be noted, did not have a say. The oath of allegiance to the Confederate government included the phrase: "I will in all things demean myself as a true and faithful citizen." Someone was appointed to each Southern county to administer this oath.

Aside from slavery, the other main priority for Confederates was states' rights. The framers quickly realized that they had to present a united front in order to minimize disagreement. They also, without realizing the irony of the situation, modeled their Constitution off the original one made by the Founding Fathers. If they wanted to keep a hold on slavery, they had to consolidate their power, which put the idea of states' rights on the back burner. In fact, some of the changes they made went directly against states' rights. This was government by a unified class, not government for the people.

The Confederate Constitution differed from the original in a few key ways. The original US system of government, like the current one, included three branches—the executive, legislative, and judicial—and included checks and balances to ensure that no one branch had too much power. The Confederate government did not include a judicial branch, as the Confederate congress elected not to establish a Supreme Court. Individual states still had their own court systems, but appeals processes were more difficult (or impossible) because higher courts in most cases did not exist. Lower courts could only do so much if there was no higher court.

The framers of the Confederate Constitution also served in the provisional Congress, meaning that they had the power to decide what laws would be passed under the document that they themselves had written. This was another absence of checks and balances.

When the framers put together the original US Constitution, they intentionally made it somewhat fungible, leaving room for future generations to interpret or change it as they saw necessary. The Confederate government did not want to allow that because they did not want any disagreement holding them up. The US Constitution's position on slavery was hazy. The Confederates purposely left no room for interpretation on this issue in their constution. Article IV, section 2 reads as follows: "The citizens of each State shall be entitled to all the privileges and immunities of citizens in the several States; and shall have the right of transit and sojourn in any State of this Confederacy, with their slaves and other property; and the right of property in said slaves shall not be thereby impaired."

The document also covered the possibility that slaves may escape. If one did, he or she was not to be "discharged from such service or labor, but delivered upon claim of the party to whom such slave belongs." The Confederate constitution also protected the institution of slavery in any future territory the Confederacy might acquire.

Conscription, or the ability to draft citizens into service in the military, was not allowed in the original US Constitution. It just allowed for Congress "to provide for calling forth the Militia to execute the Laws of the Union, suppress Insurrections and repel Invasions." It did not allow the government to press people into service. The Confederate constitution did not explicitly allow conscription either.

CONSTITUTION

OF THE

CONFEDERATE STATES OF AMERICA.

WE, the people of the Confederate States, each State acting in its sovereign and independent character, in order to form a permanent federal government, establish justice, insure domestic tranquillity, and secure the blessings of liberty to ourselves and our posterity—invoking the favor and guidance of Almighty God—do ordain and establish this Constitution for the Confederate States of America.

ARTICLE I.

SECTION 1.

All legislative powers herein delegated shall be vested in a Congress of the Confederate States, which shall consist of a Senate and House of Representatives.

SECTION 2.

1. The House of Representatives shall be composed of members chosen every second year by the people of the several States; and the electors in each State shall be citizens of the Confederate States, and have the qualifications requisite for electors of the most numerous branch of the State Legislature; but no person of foreign birth, not a citizen of the Confederate States, shall be allowed to vote for any officer, civil or political, State or Federal.

2. No person shall be a Representative who shall not have attained the age of twenty-five years, and be a citizen of the Confederate States, and who shall not, when elected, be an inhabitant of that State in which he shall be chosen.

The first page of the Confederate Constitution

Initially, the Confederate army was made up of about two hundred thousand volunteers and militiamen. In March 1862, the initial volunteers' terms of service were coming to an end. President Davis sent a message to the Confederate House of Representatives clarifying that conscription would be necessary. He acknowledged that the constitution was confusing, saying:

> The frequent changes and amendments which have been made have rendered the system so complicated as to make it often quite difficult to determine what the law really is." He continued, "in order to maintain this reserve intact, it is necessary that, in a great war like that in which we are now engaged, all persons of intermediate age not legally exempt for good cause

Secession Map

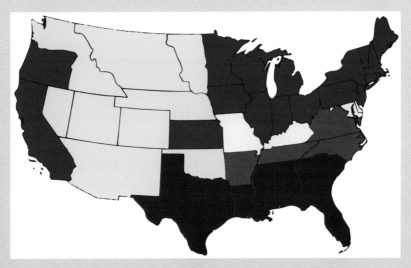

The United States in 1861. The states shown in red seceded from the Union (blue) on the dates below. The states in yellow allowed slavery but remained in the Union.

South Carolina: December 20, 1860

Mississippi: January 9, 1861

Florida: January 10, 1861

Alabama: January 11, 1861

Georgia: January 19, 1861

Louisiana: January 26, 1861

Texas: February 1, 1861

Virginia: April 17, 1861

Arkansas: May 6, 1861

North Carolina: May 20, 1861

Tennessee: June 8, 1861

should pay their debt of military service to the country, that the burthens [burdens] should not fall exclusively on the most ardent and patriotic.

He concluded his letter by recommending that a bill be passed, declaring all persons between the ages of eighteen and thirty-five "rightfully subject to military duty." Shortly afterward, the Confederacy passed another law that mandated all soldiers to remain enlisted for the duration.

The Confederacy asserted its independence in a few other key ways in its constitution. There was no federally aided growth allowed. The Confederates wanted their economy to be entirely agricultural, without the influence of manufacturing or government aid. They saw this, "taking the money out of politics," as a step away from democracy and the class conflict that they believed came with democracy. Additionally, non-Southerners, or "foreigners," were not allowed to vote.

The framers chose their colleagues, Jefferson Davis and Alexander Stephens, for president and vice president of the new nation. In the Confederate constitution, the president and vice president were allowed one six-year term.

The new nation hoped that the North would accept its breaking off peacefully. According to some historians, they did not necessarily want a war; they just wanted to form their own government. Most secessionists would probably agree that they wanted to secede for the issue of states' rights. The Confederacy had also started to take over federal facilities in Southern states. They took over a Pensacola

The first battle of the Civil War occurred at Fort Sumter, in Charleston Harbor.

navy yard and seized a New Orleans customs house in January 1861, before Lincoln's inauguration and before the Confederacy had officially formed. The federal government saw these facilities as still being federal property. In April, when Confederate troops took over Fort Sumter in the harbor of Charleston, South Carolina, the Union saw this as the "last straw."

Lincoln quickly called for seventy-five thousand volunteers to serve for three months fighting the Confederacy. The South's hopes for a peaceful acceptance of their new national identity were gone. Once the war began, border states had to decide where their loyalties lay. Virginia, North Carolina, Tennessee, and Arkansas joined the Confederacy. Maryland and Delaware had been slave states but joined the Union.

A painting from 1869 by
Everett B. D. Julio of Lee with
General Stonewall Jackson

The Making of the Face of the Confederacy

L ee might have said that he was a Virginian before he was an American. It's also been said that "he came out of his mother's womb a soldier." His great-great grandfather Richard "The Emigrant" Lee had arrived in Jamestown around 1640. The Lee family had been an established Virginia family ever since.

Lee's Parentage and the Washington Connection

Lee's grandfather, Henry Lee II, married a woman named Lucy Grymes. Lucy happened to be a young George Washington's first romantic interest. She did not return Washington's favors, maybe because he did not have much to offer in the way of prospects. He was only eighteen and did not even own a home yet. Henry and Lucy Lee had a son, also named Henry (or Harry), who would go on to fight in the Revolutionary War under Washington. This soldier, Harry, was Robert E. Lee's father.

Harry attended Princeton, then called the College of New Jersey. Shortly after graduating in 1773, he had plans to pursue a law degree in London, but he instead joined the fight for American independence. He received a commission as a captain in the dragoons. Dragoons, unlike cavalry, were soldiers who rode on horseback but dismounted to fight. Unlike his son Robert, Harry Lee lived for combat and confrontation and became somewhat of a legend. At one point, the British army sent three hundred men to capture Lee, dead or alive, at the Spread Eagle Tavern near Valley Forge. Lee fought them off, partly by bluffing that he had reinforcements on the way. He didn't, but the British didn't want to take the chance, so they retreated. By this point, the young captain had already acquainted himself with General Washington, but this earned him a letter of congratulations from the general. It also earned him an invitation to be part of Washington's military family as a staff officer working on correspondence. Lee didn't want to have an office job. Washington then made another offer, making Lee the commander of "two troops of horse." Lee was twenty-two, and it was then that he earned the nickname "Light Horse Harry." These one hundred horsemen operated outside the direct chain of command. Lee foraged for materials, often stealing from the British. Food and medicine that he stole helped keep Washington and his troops alive at Valley Forge.

Toward the end of the war, Harry persuaded the commander of the American theater of operations, Nathaniel Greene, to lead an offensive into South Carolina. This was at the same time as the British, under Charles Cornwallis, were heading to Virginia. This pinned the British in Yorktown, where they surrendered to Washington. Lee got to see it firsthand.

Twenty-six-year-old Harry chose not to remain a soldier, and he went on to make a series of poor decisions. Washington was engaged in a project to build a canal on the Potomac River that bypassed Great Falls for more ease of commerce connecting east and west. Lee bought five hundred acres of land around the falls, believing that the area would soon be bustling with commerce. The profits never came, and the plan did not go forward as Washington had been so confident it would. Lee never did pay off his debt to Washington.

Harry Lee also had a hand in shaping the young country's government. After the Constitutional Convention, each state had to agree to ratify the document at its own convention. In Virginia, Lee did his part to push for ratification. He related to his delegates that he felt the strength of the Union by fighting alongside Northerners during the Revolution: "I love the people of the North, not because they have adopted the Constitution; but, because I fought with them as my countrymen, and because I consider them as such. Does it follow from hence, that I have forgotten my attachment to my native State? In all local matters I shall be a Virginian: In those of a general nature, I shall not forget that I am an American." Harry's son would eventually face a similar question of whether to be loyal to his state or to his country. Harry Lee also advocated for Washington to be the first president.

Washington died just weeks before the turn of the nineteenth century. Harry got to deliver his eulogy, with the familiar phrase "first in war, first in peace, and first in the heart of his countrymen." Washington did not live to meet Harry's son Robert, but the personality of Washington hung over Robert E. Lee for his whole life, partly because of his father's connection to Washington and partly because of the woman he would marry.

Anne Carter Lee, Robert's mother, was Harry's second wife. Harry had previously been married to a woman named Matilda, who died in 1790 after having four children. Robert was Anne's fifth child, making him his father's ninth. Robert did not get to know his father much, because Harry spent a year in a debtors' prison while Robert was a toddler. In 1810, the Lee family could no longer afford to stay at the Stratford House where Robert had been born, and they moved to Alexandria, Virginia. In 1812, Harry and other Federalists believed that Thomas Jefferson, James Madison, and other populists were pushing the country into another war with Britain. A friend of Harry's, Alexander Hanson, had similar opinions and used his newspaper in Baltimore to publish them. A populist mob stormed the newspaper office, and Harry went to support his friend. Things got so violent that the populists literally tore the building down. Even after Harry and the other Federalists were locked up in jail, the populists continued to beat them. One person died, and Harry received such awful injuries that the mob believed him to be dead.

Harry returned home heavily mutilated, and this was the first time that his five-year-old son Robert remembered seeing him. Harry spent the rest of his life ill and in debt. After failing to show up in court at one point, he left for the West Indies and did not return to the United States until he felt he was dying. He did not make it home, though—he died in 1818 on Cumberland Island, Georgia. At this time, Robert was eleven years old.

A Young Soldier and Father

Robert E. Lee's older brothers went away to college and the military. With the absence of his father, Lee effectively became the man of the house. Anne had many health problems, and he took care of her until he went to college.

Lee's older brother had attended Harvard, but by the time Lee reached college-bound age, his family could not afford to send him there. He attended West Point from 1825 to 1829, graduating second in his class with a spotless disciplinary record. Upon graduating, he received a commission as a lieutenant in the Corps of Engineers. Also in 1829, his mother died, so he briefly returned to help sort out her affairs. He then began a seventeen-month appointment, supervising the building of Fort Pulaski on Cockspur Island, Georgia.

During a hiatus from this appointment, Lee spent time with his mother's cousin's family, the Custis family, on their Virginia plantation, Arlington. Lee and the

Arlington House in 1864, once the Union government had bought it from the Lees

daughter of this family, Mary Randolph Custis, had played together as children. In their adulthood, Lee took a fancy to her. They married at Arlington a few months after Lee proposed in 1831.

If the name Arlington sounds familiar, it's because this is the same piece of land that is now known as Arlington National Cemetery. If the name Custis sounds familiar, it's because the family were descendants of Martha Custis Washington, George Washington's wife.

The Lees had seven children together between the years of 1832 and 1846. His sons were named George Washington Custis, who was called Custis; William Henry Fitzhugh, who went by Rooney; and Robert Edward, simply known as Rob. His daughters were Mary Custis, named after her mother; Anne Carter, or Annie; Eleanor Agnes, known as Agnes; and the youngest, Mildred Childe. It was not conventional for an army officer to bring his family with him wherever he went, so Lee probably spent more time away from his family than he did with them. He undoubtedly remembered his own childhood without a father, so he underwent a lot of anxiety about how he could properly fulfill his fatherly duties. He saw those duties to be, principally, guiding his children to be morally well-formed adults who would bring continued honor to the family name. His philosophy was that of strict discipline, occasionally tempered with kindness and affection. Since he was often not there to administer it, he sent detailed directives in letters to Mary, perhaps not believing that her perspective as the full-time parent might grant her some knowledge on the subject as well.

The fact that he had no father figure as a model occasionally showed through in his communication with his children. He pushed his eldest son Custis especially hard, because Custis racked up several demerits at West Point and eventually got in trouble for having alcohol in his room. No matter how hard Custis tried, it was never enough for his father, who urged him in letters, "You must be No. 1. It is a fine number … Jump to it fellow." In the eighteenth century, children were often seen as existing for their parents, not just for themselves. The children were the ones who would either uphold or tarnish the family name. In one letter to his mother-in-law, he wrote, "God punishes us for our

Mary Lee lived on for a few years after her husband but never quite recovered from losing Arlington.

sins here and hereafter. He is now punishing me for mine through my children." One can only wonder what Mary would have to say to this.

Lee's first assignment after his marriage was at Fort Monroe, in Virginia. He became quite the nomadic creature for the next fifteen years until the war with Mexico. Despite being a commissioned officer for all that time, Lee's work had only focused on engineering and infrastructure. The Mexican war would be his first exposure to combat. He was put on Brigadier General John E. Wool's staff as an engineer, but in January of the following year, he was reassigned. His new commander, Major General Winfield Scott, served as Lee's mentor.

During this war, Lee's work consisted of some engineering work, directing the construction of gun emplacements and reconnoitering on horseback, often riding 50 to 60 miles (80 to 97 km) a day. He took part in the siege of Vera Cruz. As mentioned, General Scott admired Lee's aptitude. Lee met several others during this war that he would work with (or against) in the future, including P.G.T. Beauregard, a future Confederate general. Lee and Beauregard were nearly shot by other US soldiers who mistook them for Mexican soldiers. He also briefly met Ulysses Grant, who would become his Union counterpart years in the future.

When the war ended with Mexico's surrender in 1848, Lee returned home to Arlington, but not for long. He resumed the engineering life, overseeing the construction of Fort Carroll in Baltimore from 1848 to 1852. In the fall of 1852, he became superintendent at West Point. Among others, Lee answered to then-secretary of war Jefferson Davis, who would later become the president of the Confederacy.

In 1855, however, Lee received new orders again. He had to move to Camp Cooper, Texas, where he was put in charge of two squadrons of the Second Cavalry, again outside of his engineering comfort zone. Part of the job involved protecting settlers in the newly annexed Texas from Native Americans. During this time, the Lee family experienced several hardships. Lee's younger sister died, as did Mary's father. As his sole heir, Mary inherited the Arlington estate and Lee became the executor, which was quite a burden. Lee had to take several leaves from his duty to attend to Arlington. The estate needed much repair and more money than the family had. They were able to hold onto it, mostly due to gifts from family members. Lee's next assignment was putting down John Brown's rebellion.

Lee's Civil War: The Beginning

While he said that he much preferred to be in the field with soldiers, Lee began the war as an advisor to the Confederate president, Jefferson Davis, in Richmond. He did not go near a battlefield until August, when Davis dispatched him to settle disputes in western Virginia.

At the time, modern-day Virginia and West Virginia were one state, but Union sympathies were high in the western area. West Virginians had elected their own governor and declared the secessionist regime illegal. Union General McClellan came with his troops and pushed Confederate troops back to the east. It was this Union-leaning climate that Davis sent Lee into, and Lee's main objective was to stop the Union from entering the Shenandoah Valley. The Shenandoah Valley was called the "breadbasket of the Confederacy," and control of it also meant control of several mountain passes. President Davis did not grant Lee decisive authority; he instead sent Lee to help supervise and assist Brigadier General William Loring, whose soldiers were camped at Huntersville, North Carolina.

Lee and his army spent about a month in terrible weather, scouting and engaging in some skirmishes with the Union, but no full-on battle happened. His troops also suffered many illnesses. He wrote that "those on the sick list would form an army" themselves. The battle finally happened on September 12. Lee's battle plan involved coordinating multiple columns of men on the sides of a mountain, Cheat Mountain. His men on the east side of Cheat Mountain were supposed to signal with gunfire that they were ready to attack. The soldier that Lee had appointed to this task lost his nerve at the last minute. The troops on the west side never heard the nonexistent gunfire, so they did not proceed with the attack, and the element of surprise was lost.

The loss at Cheat Mountain, and several subsequent Confederate losses, earned Lee the nickname "Granny" in the papers, as people believed him to be a timid leader. He was cautious, but the loss at Cheat Mountain was also precipitated by a series of miscommunications, some of which were not his fault.

The Middle

For about four months starting in November 1861, Lee commanded the Department of South Carolina, Georgia, and Florida, protecting the coastal forts. From March until May 1862, he was back in Richmond advising Davis. In May, he received an assignment to fill in for the injured Joseph E. Johnston, commanding the Army of Northern Virginia. He expected to return to Richmond as soon as Johnston recovered from his injury, but he stayed with the Army of Northern Virginia for the remainder of the war. It was here that Lee began the part of his career for which he is best known; it also meant that he wouldn't keep the nickname "Granny" much longer.

Lee's reputation improved with a series of battles on the Virginia peninsula known as the Seven Days' Battles. The Confederacy suffered more casualties than the Union did. The Battle of Second Manassas (Second Bull Run) on August 29 was another win for the Confederacy. Lee suffered an injury following the battle. He fell, spraining one hand and breaking several bones in another. He couldn't ride for two weeks.

In early September, Lee executed what is now called the Maryland Campaign. He wanted to head north to bring the war away from Virginia, to disrupt the east/west railway line, and to perhaps gain support from Confederate-leaning citizens in Maryland. He wrote a proclamation to the citizens of Maryland, asking the Northern states to "allow the Confederacy to exist in peace," and that "the Confederacy has been forced to invade to defend citizens and property." This did not work out as he had hoped. A Union soldier found a copy of Lee's battle plans, but fortunately for Lee, the Union general was cautious and did not move right away. The Confederate army split in two: General Thomas

"Stonewall" Jackson went to take over Harpers Ferry, and Lee fought off federal forces near Sharpsburg.

Sharpsburg was the location of the bloodiest single battle of the war, known to Northerners as the Battle of Antietam. Apparently during the battle, Lee was walking in the town of Sharpsburg and ran into a battery of young Confederate soldiers. One of these soldiers was his son, Rob. Lee chatted with the young men for a while but did not recognize Rob until Rob identified himself.

The battle at Sharpsburg was a Confederate loss. With 2,700 men killed, 9,024 wounded, and 2,000 missing, Lee suffered 26 percent casualties. Union General George McClellan suffered 16 percent. Given the loss at Antietam, the Maryland campaign was not a success for Lee. On December 13, the Battle of Fredericksburg was a Confederate win.

In January 1863, Lee's men were camped along the Rappahannock River. Especially in winter, the soldiers suffered greatly for lack of food, supplies, horses, and artillery. There are stories of men having to march miles without shoes, and of Lee's son Rob approaching him and asking for a pair of shoes. Lee told him instead to wait until his regiment had gotten the go-ahead for new shoes. Mary Lee showed her support by knitting socks and sending them Lee's way. These socks became a recurring theme in their letters to each other. Throughout the war, the Confederate troops were underfed and poorly supplied, partly because their railroad connections were often cut off. They relied heavily on food sent from home. The Union army had assistance from the Sanitary Commission for food and medical care, but the

Confederates did not have this. Long stretches in winter camp took severe tolls on the men's morale.

Meanwhile, the Union army had replaced General Burnside with General Hooker. Hooker created a lot of noise up and down the Rappahannock, but Lee knew he would not move until spring. He wrote to his daughter Agnes, "General Hooker is obliged to do something. I do not know what it will be … He runs out his guns, starts his wagons and troops up and down the river, and creates an excitement generally."

On April 29, Hooker crossed the river, initiating the Battle of Chancellorsville. While out scouting after dark, Stonewall Jackson was mistakenly shot by one of his men. He lost his arm and died about a week later of pneumonia. Lee was devastated—before Jackson died, he wrote to him that he wished it had been him. Even so, Chancellorsville was a Confederate victory.

In May, the war clerk asked Lee to send some troops to Vicksburg, Mississippi, as Grant was holding the town under siege. Lee declined, wanting to protect Virginia. He then decided to go north again, to Pennsylvania, to draw attention away from his home state, and to go on the offensive. Lee's colleague, General Longstreet, found out from a scout that the Union command had changed again, from Hooker to Meade. He also learned that the Union army appeared to have concentrated at Gettysburg, Pennsylvania. Lee wanted to fight an offensive battle, but Longstreet disagreed and disapproved of the whole operation.

During the three-day battle of Gettysburg, Lee was ill, possibly with malaria. Historians suggest that he still had the Battle of Chancellorsville in his mind, where the Army of Northern Virginia had been sorely outnumbered and still came out victorious. At Gettysburg, for the first time in a while, Lee's men were about equal in number to those of the rival army, the Army of the Potomac.

Once at Gettysburg, Longstreet again made a suggestion. He suggested moving to another field, in order to encourage the Union to attack, but Lee did not do this.

During the second day of battle, Lee still believed his men would come out on top. The third day of battle was by far the worst. Longstreet commanded three divisions, the strongest being General George Pickett's thirteen thousand Virginia men. On Lee's orders, they charged Meade's center on Cemetery Hill. After a disastrous hour of artillery fire, Pickett's men retreated. Meanwhile, eastward, General Jeb Stuart's cavalry were beaten as well.

Lee remained quite passive, yet resolute, in his decisions at Gettysburg. Arthur J.L. Fremantle, a British soldier who witnessed Gettysburg, observed Lee's leadership style during the battle: "It is evidently his system to arrange the plan thoroughly with the three corps commanders, and then to leave to them the duty of modifying and carrying it out to the best of their abilities." After the battle, Lee remained a strong face for his men, and told one general, "It is I that have lost this fight, and you must help me out of it the best way you can."

In future letters, Lee would blame several other people for the loss: General Stuart and his cavalry took a long time to circumvent the Union army during a scouting mission, and therefore arrived late to the battle with no intelligence for Lee. Additionally, Lee's army ran out of ammunition earlier than the Union army did, and he blamed this on the artillery commander. Longstreet also became a scapegoat, perhaps unfairly, as his advice was not taken.

Lee lost one third of his army at Gettysburg. Lee would also write to President Davis twice after Gettysburg, both times asking to be relieved of his command. Both times, Davis declined the request.

The End

Following Gettysburg, Lee changed tactics and fought much more defensively. The "go for broke" offensive moves that brought him to Gettysburg had not paid off, and he had learned his lesson.

On the same day that the Union won at Gettysburg, Grant was victorious, as the siege of Vicksburg came to an end.

In May 1864, Grant took control of the whole Union army. Eventually, Lee's operations devolved into doing anything to stop Grant from getting to Richmond, the capital. The war dragged on for another year. In February 1865, the Confederate congress wanted to create a position of general-in-chief of all armies, the position that Grant had in the Union army. Until now, President Davis had effectively been the general-in-chief. He appointed Lee as the general-in-chief of all Confederate armies in an act of desperation.

In another act of desperation, the Confederacy decided to allow freed slaves to serve as soldiers. Lee and others encouraged this, despite pushback from Davis. A law made it legal to emancipate slaves if they became soldiers, but

A few Confederate volunteers in Pensacola, Florida, in 1861

This lithograph by Currier and Ives shows Richmond on fire on the night of April 2, 1865.

this happened only a few months before the war's end. Not much came of it.

In February, General William T. Sherman, Grant's right-hand man, was executing his March to the Sea. Having destroyed Atlanta, he moved in the direction of Savannah, destroying train tracks, forts, and bridges. Lee asked Joseph E. Johnston to assume command of the armies of Tennessee, South Carolina, Georgia, and Florida, to do whatever he could to push back Sherman. Johnston replied that it was too late for this.

The final nail in the coffin for the Confederacy was that the Union seized the Southside Railroad. This meant that Petersburg and Richmond had to be evacuated. Families headed south by train. Confederate soldiers started an "evacuation fire" in Richmond so that at least Union forces wouldn't be able to stock up on the town's remaining cotton and supplies.

Lee decided that it would be "useless and therefore cruel to provoke the further effusion of blood, and I have arranged to meet with General Grant." Soon, Lee and Grant were exchanging letters. The first came from Grant, suggesting a surrender. Their interview occurred on April 9, in the Wilmer McLean House, in the town of Appomattox Court House, Virginia. Grant's terms were described as generous, allowing Lee's soldiers to be paroled and head home with their belongings.

Lee's soldiers were of course upset to hear of the surrender, but they did not begrudge their fearless leader. They expressed sympathy for him, and even a willingness to keep fighting. Toward the end of the war, they had been fighting for him as much as for anything else. Two days after the surrender, Lee headed to Richmond to rejoin his family.

At several points during the war, Lee allowed his loyalty to Virginia to guide his decisions on where to send his army. Would things have turned out differently had he not had this bias?

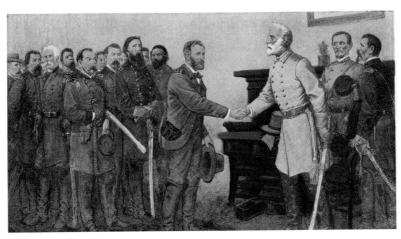

A postcard of Lee's surrender with art by Thomas Nast

Thomas "Stonewall" Jackson

Generals Jackson (*left*) and Lee with their respective troops, meeting for the last time before Jackson's untimely death

Lee spoke very highly of his colleague "Stonewall" Jackson. A good seventeen years younger than Lee, Jackson did not come from wealthy beginnings. He was orphaned as a child and struggled academically at West Point. He served in the War with Mexico, and it was there that he joined the Presbyterian Church. Much like Lee, Jackson was averse to smoking, drinking, and gambling.

The Stonewall Brigade earned its nickname at the Battle of First Manassas (Bull Run). His men nearly pushed another Confederate brigade out of the way, and its commander, Brigadier General Barnard E. Bee, exclaimed: "Look at Jackson's brigade; it stands like a stone wall! Rally behind the Virginians." They earned their nickname at Manassas, but they had been together since the beginning of the war, before Jackson's promotion to general. The brigade, made of five regiments of men from the Shenandoah Valley, proved to be a force of nature in several battles, including Sharpsburg, Fredericksburg, and Chancellorsville.

The Stonewall Brigade did not become what it was by accident. According to Confederate soldier Sam Watkins, Jackson's discipline was unflinching: "He would have a man shot at the drop of a hat, and drop it himself."

Jackson met an early death during the Battle of Chancellorsville. Scouting at night, he surprised some of his own men, who fired shots that landed in his right arm. His arm had to be amputated, and he died nine days later from pneumonia. Lee would later remark that in losing Jackson, he had lost his right arm as well.

The Confederacy won the
Battle of Chancellorsville on
May 4, 1863.

Lee the Traitor, Lee the Beloved

Rebel. This is the name that Union soldiers gave Confederates, and the name that Confederate soldiers proudly claimed for themselves. The Confederate spirit was rebellious, and the whole undertaking of the war from the Southern side was nothing short of rebellion. Even though Lee was the face of the Confederate cause by the end of the war, the label of "rebel" doesn't seem to fit him personally.

For Lee, the Civil War was not a war of rebellion. He joined the cause out of loyalty to Virginia—any rebellion was an unfortunate side effect. Lee had hoped that Virginia would not secede, because he did not think secession was wise. He did not want the country to go to war. Lee is a hero to some people even today. To others, he is the opposite. People's reasons for revering or resenting someone are not always based in fact.

Victorian Manhood and Lee's Ancestry

It would be unfair to judge Lee, or anyone from the nineteenth century, by twenty-first century standards. In order to assess whether Lee was a hero or villain, it's important to understand the standards of the time, and the rules of the world that he lived in.

Lee came from a family that had been called one of the "first families of Virginia." Lee's father, and later his half-brother, would make some decisions that would tarnish the family name. Harry Lee lived the latter part of his life in debt and, later, in self-imposed exile. In 1787, when his father died, Harry inherited the Stratford plantation, where Robert would later be born. In 1787, the plantation contained 6,595 acres. By 1800, the plantation had been reduced to about a tenth of its original size, because Harry kept selling off portions of it to pay for his poorly conceived business ventures. He also mortgaged the same pieces of land several times and wrote bad checks.

Harry's son from his first marriage, Henry, inherited the greatly diminished Stratford. He soon earned the nickname "Black Horse Harry." After he (like his father) spent a lot of his inheritance, he impregnated his wife's younger sister, Betsy, when he was supposed to be the young woman's guardian. Betsy lost the baby and then sued Harry to regain her estate. The county took Stratford away from Harry and eventually sold it to Betsy. He tried to obtain a diplomatic position in Algiers. Betsy continued her revenge and told John Tyler, then a member of the Virginia senate, about

Harry's abuse of her. Soon, the whole senate heard, and they denied Harry's request of the diplomatic job. He went abroad anyway and died in exile.

When he was quite young, Robert E. Lee learned of his father and his older half-brother losing their money and their honor. He knew that he was from a family that had once been great, but now had very little, and had some unfortunate stories attached to it. Knowing this may have motivated Lee to be on his best behavior growing up. He may have wanted to restore the family's name, or at least prove to others that he was virtuous and not like his delinquent relatives.

While Lee's family was not wealthy by the time he came along, he was raised nonetheless to be a Virginia gentleman. Such a gentleman was expected to exercise restraint, to not be selfish, to be disciplined, and to deny oneself. For people of Lee's parents' generation, simply being born into a family of stature would command a certain amount of respect and a high social standing. The same was still true when Lee was coming of age, but Lee also had to deal with the reputations left by his father and by Black Horse Harry. Lee's later religious conversion in 1853 enhanced his devotion to duty and his neglect of the self. He joined the Evangelical Episcopalian church with his wife, who was also a reborn Christian.

When Lee was seventeen, his uncle, William Henry Fitzhugh, who had helped take care of Lee's mother and the family after Light Horse Harry left, wrote a letter recommending Lee for admission at West Point. In this letter to the then-secretary of war John C. Calhoun, Fitzhugh did not mention his nephew's educational aptitude or experience, only his family background and character. These were the social priorities of the time, and Fitzhugh's letter worked.

The "Fine" Man

Pick up any biography of Lee, and you'll be hard-pressed not to run across a mention of his good looks. This is not a rational thing, nor is it a measure by which to judge someone's character, but people care about it nevertheless. Most popular images of Lee are from his years as General Lee, when his hair had turned gray and he looked somewhat grandfatherly. He looks stately and composed in those images, authoritative and not overpowering. This may have been the right balance for the newspaper-reading public. When Lee was young, though, he had thick dark hair, a full beard and mustache, and deep brown eyes. He stood close to six feet, tall for the time. Roy Blount Jr. opens his biography of Lee by saying that he may have been "the most beautiful person in America, a sort of precursor-cross between England's Cary Grant and Virginia's Randolph Scott." In the same book, Blount repeatedly uses the word "fine" to describe Lee, applying it not only to his looks, but to his demeanor and the way he carried himself.

Biographers also often describe Lee as having been a ladies' man. He reportedly enjoyed dancing, parties, and chatting with women, even after he was married. He was the paragon of the Virginia gentleman. Author Mary Chesnut wrote a passage recounting seeing General Lee for the first time while taking some air with a friend. This was shortly after the war began:

Robert E. Lee as a young lieutenant, age thirty-one. Biographers often remark on his handsomeness.

He sat his horse gracefully, and he was so distinguished at all points that I very much regretted not catching the name as Mrs. Stanard gave it to us. He, however, heard ours and bowed as gracefully as he rode, and the few remarks he made to each of us showed he knew all about us … Perfection— no fault to be found if you hunted for one.

Chesnut later noted in her diary that she preferred his brother, Smith Lee, because she knew him well and "like[d] his looks."

Lee's personality was one of humility and modesty. These were appreciated virtues of the time, but still he stood out as an attractive specimen to his peers in this way. During his life before the Civil War, his life was hardly his own—he was following orders. The humility pairs with the sense of duty, which was also expected of men of his station. All his life, Lee did not put himself first, often because that simply wasn't an option. He grew up mostly without a father. Once his older brothers left home, it fell mostly to Lee to take care of his mother, keeping her company as well as acting as a nurse at times. When he left for college, Mrs. Lee is reported to have remarked that Robert was "son, daughter, and everything to me!" As a young engineer for the army, he traveled to wherever he was assigned, often spending long stretches away from his wife and children. When faced with the choice to defend the country or the state of Virginia, he stuck with the one that he had been taught to be loyal to, even though he personally disagreed with his own state's decision to secede. Whether or not one agrees with Lee's decisions or morals, one has to acknowledge that he was not a self-centered person, making him an attractive figure during his lifetime and even more so after.

During the war, his humility shone through in quotidian actions such as eating from tin dishes, instead of china, and sleeping in tents or under the stars. Only when he experienced a bout of rheumatism in late 1863 did he start to sleep in a house. He kept chickens in camp and loved to ride his horse, Traveller. Historians have noted a small mistake with Lee's uniform, which may have been charming to his compatriots: on his collar, he wore the three stars of colonel, a rank he had surpassed. The correct insignia for a Confederate general was three stars within a wreath. Small characteristics like this may have allowed his many soldiers to feel as though he was on their level, and that he sympathized with them. People longed for a leader whom they felt was one of them.

Lee is mostly known for being on the "wrong" side, or depending on one's point of view, the "losing" side of the War Between the States. The fact that he lost the war did not tarnish his reputation among those who had already decided they loved him. Becoming the face of the losing side was the perfect platform for Lee's already well-developed disposition as someone who does not put himself first, but someone who is stoic and humble. To people who were already fans of Lee, his loss only made him more endearing.

In Civil War terminology, the phrase "Lost Cause" has come to identify not just a lost war, but a lost way of life. The South's reliance on agriculture and slavery was

A woodcut of Lee, with the three stars on his collar signifying the rank of colonel, not general

Robert E. Lee: Commander of the Confederate Army

essentially giving way to the industrialism of the North. Wealthy Southerners—the planter class—did not want to lose that way of life. It is more difficult to know what lower-class Southerners thought of Lee, because they weren't the ones whose voices were being heard in the Confederate government. Even if secession and war were mostly acting in the service of wealthy slave owners, poorer whites may still have clung to the idea of Lee as the Virginian who took a stand for his state to keep Northern influence away.

Man Becomes Myth

After Lee died, he was nearly idolized and eventually became a canvas onto which people could project their feelings after the harrowing war. Many people named their sons after him. Glowing biographies, depicting him as a near-saint, began to come out. Other previous Confederate officers defended Lee and wrote of his greatness in letters and articles. The Lee Memorial Foundation worked on building a permanent tomb and monument. At the suggestion of Mary Custis Lee, a larger-than-life statue was built, costing $15,000 (just over $347,000 in modern day currency), depicting Lee asleep on the field of battle. By 1883, the mausoleum and statue were complete. Nearly ten thousand people gathered at the Washington and Lee campus for the unveiling. Former Confederate general Jubal Early presided over the ceremony. Shortly after this event, Lee began to loom large in the Lost Cause imagery, again like a saint.

Believers in the Lost Cause believed that the South would have won the war if the North did not have more industry and more men on its side. They were quick to say

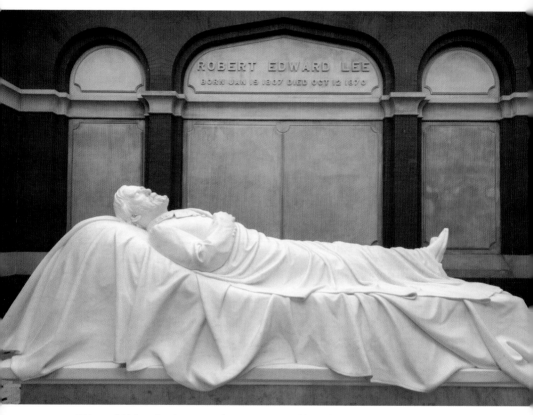

Edward Valentine's recumbent statue of Lee in the chapel on the
Washington and Lee campus. Lee's horse, Traveller, is buried on the
premises as well.

that Lee did not lose the war; he surrendered, reinforcing the idea of Lee as a gentlemanly figure. They quickly developed a nostalgic view of the antebellum South. One needs only to listen to the opening lines of "Dixie" to get a taste of the nostalgia: "Well I wish I was in the land of cotton; old times there were not forgotten! Look away, look away, look away, Dixieland!"

The Lost Cause myth was connected to another myth, that of the Southern cavalier—a member of the planter class who was seen as an elite, refined individual, very much tied to the plantation way of life. Lee was a prime embodiment of the Southern cavalier mythology. The idea of the Southern cavalier was very comforting to people before and during the war, but especially after. After the war, once it was clear that plantations were going to die out, the Southern cavalier became a comforting image, and a nostalgic reminder of an era that would not last. They were seen as a bastion of stability, even in the climate of immigration and industrialization that was starting to creep down from the North.

It was not only in the South that Lee turned into a hero, however. Shortly after his death, the Northern press also began to preach the gospel of Lee. Northerners were as intrigued by the Southern cavalier mythology as the Southerners were attached to it. He was often characterized as above the controversy, not attached to the atrocities of war or the institution of slavery. The *New York Times*'s obituary of Lee wrote that his decision to align himself with the Confederacy was an "error of judgment." Even if they didn't share his ideals, Northerners were happy to accept a portrait of someone who was high-minded and

A tobacco package label from 1865. As the South mourned its loss, it held on to the image of Lee and the honor that he represented.

fair, and who struggled between allegiance to his country or his state. The magic of nostalgia worked in the North as well as in the South.

Lee lived on after the war for five years, but many of the men under his command weren't so lucky. While he had to spend years away from his own family during his career, he could have been said to be a patriarch figure for his soldiers. Since so many young men died, their families may have looked to the figure of Lee for comfort. Lee became the face of the Confederacy and the face of the idea that their sons, husbands, and brothers had not died for nothing.

Lee the Villain

Newspapers and magazines that portrayed "Lee the traitor" emphasized not his character or his personality, but his connections to the war and slavery.

By the end of the war, the fact that Lee was the face of the entire Confederacy is enough for some people to consider him a villain. His relationship with slavery, though, is the sticking point for a lot of people. As historian Peter Carmichael puts it, it is "the flint that refuses to go dull," and time and time again, it has landed Lee in the villain column.

One biographer, Elizabeth Brown Pryor, notes that historians tend to ignore Lee's connections with slavery, or sometimes assert that he said nothing of consequence about it. Pryor points out that this is not true: Lee wrote plenty of letters, still available today, that voice his opinions about slavery.

Lee was a soldier, but he was not fighting for or against slavery. As Pryor puts it, he "acquiesced" to it. His family was not particularly wealthy, but they did own some slaves. They moved to Alexandria, Virginia, when Lee was young, and Alexandria was a main hub of the slave trade. When Lee's mother died, he inherited the slaves attached to her household. This was a small family, consisting of a woman named Nancy and her children. Since Lee did not feel the need to have slaves in his household, or while he was living in tents engineering, Lee rented the family out. This was relatively common practice at the time. He did make sure that they stayed together as a family, but there is no record that he emancipated them.

Lee became the executor of the Arlington estate when his father-in-law died in 1855. Lee's parents-in-law had inherited several hundred slaves from Martha Custis Washington, and those slaves came with the estate. The Arlington estate was a well-known household, and its retention of slavery was starting to attract negative attention from abolitionists.

In his will, Lee's father-in-law specified that the slaves at Arlington should be freed, but only said that it should be done within five years. The will also left legacies to Lee's daughters, but the money for those legacies did not exist. The will specified that some of the thousands of acres of Arlington land could be sold to pay for these legacies. Lee followed neither of these instructions. He interpreted the will as meaning that he could keep the slaves on until the estate made enough money to pay for the legacies. He also tried to make a little more money by hiring out his slaves to other plantations, sometimes hundreds of miles away. Since Lee usually hired the slaves out individually, many families were broken up in the process.

Lee realized eventually that the legacies would not be paid in five years, but he still did not want to sell the land. He petitioned a local court to allow him to keep the slaves enslaved as long as he needed to pay the inheritances. He also asked for permission to hire the slaves out to out-of-state plantations. The court ruled against him, so he appealed to a higher court. This continued until 1862, and the higher court ruled against him as well, directing Lee to emancipate all his slaves by the first of the next year. Ultimately, Lee had to sell Arlington in order to pay for his daughters' inheritance. Had he done so much sooner, he would not have kept so many people enslaved for so long. In January 1864, the Lincoln administration bought the Arlington house for $26,800 (roughly equal to $400,000 in modern day currency).

One can find endless anecdotes about Lee's interactions with slaves, good and bad. The most trustworthy, if not the most comprehensive, source about Lee's ideas on slavery may be his own writing. One of the most oft-quoted pieces of Lee's writing about slavery is in this 1856 letter to his wife. After the opening greetings, the letter reads as follows:

> In this enlightened age, there are few I believe, but what will acknowledge, that slavery as an institution, is a moral and political evil in any Country. It is useless to expatiate on its disadvantages. I think it however a greater evil to the white than to the black race, & while my feelings are strongly enlisted in behalf of the latter, my sympathies are more strong for the former. The blacks are immeasurably better off here than in Africa, morally, socially & physically. The painful discipline they are undergoing, is necessary for their instruction as a race, & I hope will prepare & lead them to better things. How long their subjection may be necessary is known & ordered by a wise and Merciful Providence. Their emancipation will sooner result from a mild and melting influence than the storms and contests of fiery controversy. This influence, though slow, is sure.

The doctrines and miracles of our Saviour have required nearly two thousand years to convert but a small part of the human race, and even among Christian nations what gross errors still exist! While we see the Course of the final abolition of human Slavery is onward, & we give it all the aid of our prayers & all justified means in our power, we must leave the progress as well as the result in his hands who sees the end; who Chooses to work by slow influences; & with whom two thousand years are but as a Single day; although the abolitionist must know this, and must see that he has neither the right nor power of operating except by moral means and suasion; and if he means well to the slave, he must not create angry feelings in the master. That although he may not approve the mode by which it pleases Providence to accomplish its purposes, the result will never be the same; that the reasons he gives for interference in what he has no concern hold good for every kind of interference with our neighbors when we disapprove their conduct. Is it not strange that the descendants of those Pilgrim Fathers who crossed the Atlantic to preserve the freedom of their opinion have always proved themselves intolerant of the spiritual liberty of others.

As Pryor notes, some historians have used this letter as evidence that Lee was anti-slavery. He does acknowledge that slavery is a painful and trying experience, even calling it an evil, but not because it constitutes ownership and subjugation of other human lives—because it makes white people's lives harder too. To say that slavery is more trying for the owners than for the slaves shows a basic lack of empathy. It was also a common opinion among other slave owners and founding fathers. On some level, they could see that slavery was wrong, but they could not fathom ending it, because the whole economy would have collapsed.

Lee skirts around this moral issue by leaving it up to a higher power. He does not acknowledge that slavery was one of the reasons the country was at war with itself. For Lee, this was not a war on slavery, and he did not see it as his responsibility to do anything about slavery.

Lee then turns to the abolitionists, saying that they should not anger the slave owners or create any animosity for an issue that is not of their concern. He goes so far as to equate abolitionists' ways with infringing on others' freedom of opinion. He misses the abolitionists' message. He calls slavery a "moral and political evil," but lines later, he calls abolitionists' opposition to slavery a mere "opinion."

We have to remember that "abolitionist" was not just a term for anyone who opposed slavery. It described people like William Lloyd Garrison, who advocated for ending slavery immediately. He and other abolitionists believed that such a change was not going to come about without "the storms and contests of fiery controversy," as Lee put it. The most vocal abolitionists had these militant attitudes, which further put off people like Lee, who did not care for politics or any kind of conflict. Ironically, Lee believed that a conflict would not end slavery, and that slavery was out of his hands. In truth, it did take a huge conflict to end slavery, and Lee was at the helm of this conflict.

Perhaps more damning than Lee's attitude that the injustice of slavery was out of his hands were some of his attitudes about people who were not white. During his time in Mexico, he noted in letters that the Mexican people were "a miserable populace" and "an amiable but weak people. Primitive in their habits and tastes."

His attitude towards Native Americans was even worse. When stationed in Texas, before the Civil War, he wrote home about the Comanche tribe there: "Their paints and ornaments make them more hideous than nature made them, and the whole race is extremely uninteresting." When fighting against the Comanche escalated in 1857, Lee wrote to Mary about the harsh punishments that his army had meted out. During one episode, Lee's lieutenants killed over a dozen Native Americans, wounded more, and captured their animals and equipment. "It is a distressing state of things that requires the applications of such harsh treatment, but it is the only corrective they understand & the only way in which they can be taught to keep within their own limits," he wrote.

In general, Lee's letters tell us that he saw Mexicans and black people as lesser humans, yet he saw Native Americans as even less than human. Lee seemed to ascribe to the philosophy that he, as a white man, did not need to interact with people of other races. As a white man in the nineteenth century, he was not used to having to think about people of color as people. By today's standards, this is racism.

Slavery Attitudes Surrounding Lee

Lee's mother-in-law, Mary Fitzhugh "Molly" Custis, was a big supporter of the American Colonization Society, for reasons similar to those of Robert Finley. She freed the slaves that she had inherited and persuaded her husband to free his with his will. She believed in colonization as a way around the unfortunate law that made it illegal for freed slaves to remain in Virginia. She also set up a school (likely a Sunday school) for the slaves on the Arlington property, even though it was illegal to do so. Her daughter Mary and granddaughter Agnes sometimes taught at this school.

Mary Custis Lee, Lee's wife, started out with a very optimistic view about educating slaves and had the same benevolent, if misguided, opinion on colonization as her mother. Once her father died and the slaves actually belonged to her and Lee, her attitude towards them turned less charitable. She saw owning slaves to be a real burden, and when abolitionists reportedly came to "lurk about" the property giving the slaves the idea that they should be free, she wrote: "Their freedom is a very questionable advantage to any but ourselves who will be relieved from a host of idle & their useless dependents." She could not conceive that the slaves themselves might want freedom. When Mary took a trip to Canada, where many freed and runaway slaves ended up, she noted that free blacks experienced high levels of racism and segregation. She used this to further her point that, as she wrote to one of her daughters, "I see no place for them but Africa. I am told they suffer a great deal here in the long cold winters."

Truthfully, Robert E. Lee was not a plantation owner until he and Mary inherited Arlington, at which point the task of maintaining and emancipating the slaves became a real headache. In her book *Disowning Slavery*, Joanne Pope Melish points out that many white antislavery activists were working under a disturbing pretense: "whites anticipated that free people of color, would, by some undefined moment (always imminent), have disappeared." Whites could see that slavery was wrong, but they did not care to live alongside the former enslaved people once they were freed. Some whites, such as Mary Lee, weren't antislavery at all.

Thinking back to Lee's letter to Mary, several questions arise. How much can we take someone's words at face value? How should we handle it when someone contradicts himself, as Lee does over the course of the letter? How much can he be condemned for having views that were very normal for the time? As Roy Blount Jr. wrote in his biography of Lee: "How much weight does a political statement have, when you express it only in a letter to your wife? If we found a letter from Richard Nixon to Pat in which he declares that war is evil, would we call him antiwar?" Lee made no public statements about slavery.

There's also the question of whether actions speak louder than words. As Blount puts it, in Lee's dealing with the slaves at Arlington, he was "backed into a dishonorable corner." Lee seemed not to object to freeing the slaves, but he would have lost his children's inheritance had he done so. Should he be forgiven for this?

Flag Debates

Many of people's opinions on the Confederacy come through in discussions of the Confederate battle flag. Driving through the South (and sometimes the North) in the twenty-first century, Confederate battle flags are still displayed on bumper stickers and in people's yards. In fact, there were many Confederate flags. States and regiments all had different flags that they would fly in battle. The blue cross with white stars on a red background that is seen today was the flag flown by the Army of Northern Virginia. The X-shape came from the Scottish flag of St. Andrew. This flag was never the official flag of the Confederate states.

After the war, Lee's Confederate battle flag lost most of its popularity, except during memorial events. It fell into obscurity until Strom Thurmond ran for president in 1948. The South Carolinian ran as part of the States' Rights Democratic Party, harkening back to the Civil War-era identity of the Democratic Party. As the Democrats in the nineteenth century resisted antislavery efforts, Thurmond and his party stood against the civil rights measures that the government was taking. Specifically, he stood against the antisegregation efforts. Thurmond's supporters waved the Confederate battle flag. South Carolinians also used the Confederate flag as a protest against the *Brown v. Board of Education of Topeka* Supreme Court decision, which ended segregation in public schools nationwide. To take advantage of this resurgence, enterprising merchants started to sell items featuring the Confederate battle flag, much in the same way that they sell items with the American flag on them.

The Confederate battle flag made a resurgence in 1961 and 1962, when Alabama and South Carolina raised it over their state capitol buildings to commemorate the one hundredth anniversary of the start of the Civil War. In 2000, South Carolina's state legislature enacted the Heritage Act, which stated that a two-thirds majority was needed before the flag could be removed from the capitol grounds.

In June 2015, the debate about the Confederate battle flag reached a tragic and deafening volume. A young white man shot nine people during a prayer service in a black church in Charleston, South Carolina. Since the perpetrator had previously expressed racist sentiments and taken photographs with the Confederate battle flag, citizens called for the flag to be removed from the capitol building. The following month, the legislature voted to remove the flag. The removal was accompanied by a ceremony.

All this is to say that even after this shooting and the South Carolina controversy, people still have strong opinions and disagree on the meaning of the flag. Like Lee himself, the flag served a different purpose and meant different things during the wartime than it does now. Generally, there are people who believe in the flag as an emblem of Southern pride. Others see it as directly connected to racism, slavery, and the continued oppression of black people in America. This is, admittedly, a false dichotomy: many people's views

This battle flag, never the official flag of the entire Confederacy, was flown by the Army of Northern Virginia.

on the flag do not represent either of those ends exactly. It is merely a starting point for understanding people's views on the flag.

Researchers from the University of Western Ontario conducted a qualitative study to try to get a better idea of Southerners' beliefs about the Confederate battle flag. They found that beliefs about the flag largely fell along racial lines. Of the people who saw the flag as a symbol for Southern pride, most of them were white. Of those who saw it as a racist symbol, most were black. The study only focused on Southern citizens, so it's possible that in other areas of the country, the beliefs are not as racially divided. It does make sense, since most people who fought in the Civil War were white. White people today (which may include Civil War veterans' descendants) would look more fondly upon the flag as a symbol of heritage. Many black people during the war were enslaved, and Confederate flags of all sorts represented the effort to keep them enslaved. It follows that Southern blacks today would see a very different interpretation when they look at the flag, and perhaps when they hear the name Lee.

Shifting Paradigms

Historians point out two different ways to view the past when dealing with Lee: the Victorian and the Modernist. The Victorian viewpoint is that there are clear-cut definitions of right and wrong, of "morality and immorality, and of purity and evil," as historian Carmichael puts it. These started to break down with the rise of modernism in the twentieth century, but Victorian ideals were very much alive in the nineteenth. There are still some historians today that espouse the Victorian paradigm. They are less interested in relativism and in their subjects' inner thoughts. They would rather stick to things that are proven facts.

The Modernist viewpoint is more relativist and more willing to admit that there are different definitions of right and wrong, depending on one's cultural surroundings. Modernists would advocate for evaluating Lee on his terms instead of ours. Both Modernist and Victorian thinkers can fall into the trap of emotionalism and rely more on emotion than on fact.

The conversation about Lee has been forced into a dichotomy, where people feel they have to choose between right or wrong, hero or villain. This is unfortunate and misleading, and a less intelligent way to think that does not foster new learning. Lee and the Civil War are long gone, and the US no longer practices slavery. Instead of clinging to one side of an argument, people today should actually try to learn from the past.

People for and against Lee are often evaluating him according to different criteria. Newspapers and magazines were growing in number and in readership in the mid-nineteenth century. They are useful in gauging the public opinion on Lee, both North and South. Publications tended to characterize Lee as a hero or a traitor. Those that painted him as a hero focused more on his character, personality, genetic greatness, and the fact that his father was a Revolutionary War hero. Leaders in modern times tend to be judged by their character, their political decisions, their personal convictions, and their good (or bad) looks.

Abraham Lincoln

Abraham Lincoln is mostly known for one thing today: signing the Emancipation Proclamation that freed the slaves. His untimely death by assassination likely helped to cement his reputation as a benevolent hero. Some secessionist historians, however, have grown tired of the one-dimensional view of Lincoln that is taught in schools today.

Such historians point out that, like many commanders, Lee did not see the war as a war on slavery. He did not set out to free the slaves; he set out to reclaim the states that had illegally (according to the US Constitution) broken off. Lincoln countered that illegal behavior with some illegal conduct of his own. Historian Charles Adams writes that he assumed "dictatorial powers" after the Confederates fired on Fort Sumter.

When Fort Sumter happened, Lincoln issued his call for seventy-five thousand volunteers. Adams points out that according to the Constitution, a call for troops (or "militia," as the Constitution says) requires Congressional approval, and Lincoln did not call Congress to meet until July, which was three months later. Several state governors replied that they would not be sending troops; some of these were states that would soon secede, like Virginia.

Aside from calling for volunteer troops, Lincoln called for blockades of Southern ports to cut off the South's access to trade. Blockades, as an act of war, also required Congressional approval, and Lincoln did not obtain it. Lincoln also began shutting down Southern newspapers and suspending citizens' rights of habeas corpus within weeks of Fort Sumter.

Adams argues that had Lincoln gathered Congressional approval before going on with his unilateral actions, maybe some of the states that seceded would have stayed with the Union. This is an unverifiable claim, but the takeaway here is that both Lincoln and the Confederacy viewed the other side's actions as illegal. Can laws be ignored in times of emergency? Can illegal activities be countered with more illegal activities?

An illustration of an older Robert E. Lee. Lee died in 1870 at the age of sixty-three.

J. Rogers Sc.

The Marble Model

T he "marble model," or "marble man," was the most popular nickname attached to Lee. Especially as he got older, he became more and more attached to his principles and followed them unflinchingly. Douglas Southall Freeman, author of a multivolume biography of Lee, wrote that Lee was "one of the small company of great men in whom there is no inconsistency to be explained, no enigma to be solved." In some ways, this is true: Lee was unwavering in how he never acted irrationally or out of character for himself.

Lee was not an individual without inner conflict. When Lee finally decided to fight for Virginia rather than the Union, he had to write to his old commander, Winfield Scott, and explain that he would be resigning his commission with the US

Army. After breaking the news, he wrote, "To no one, General, have I been as much indebted as to yourself for your uniform kindness and consideration, and it has always been my ardent desire to merit your approbation. I shall carry to the grave the most grateful recollections of your kind consideration, and your name and fame shall always be dear to me." The regret to be disappointing or turning against his role model was palpable. Lee took nothing lightly, especially not after turning to the Confederacy.

While he never seemed to buckle under the pressure of his heavy decisions, of losing so many men, and of being a father to seven, his inner anxiety seemed carved on his face. He likely never forgot the feeling he felt as he penned his words of regret to General Scott. Perhaps this endeared him to people, the idea that he felt life as deeply and as seriously as they did. Furthermore, he was not someone who wanted the spotlight. After the war was over, the growing press— including the Northern press—turned him into more and more of a celebrity. When he traveled by train after the war, crowds of admirers were there to meet him at the stations. His reluctance to have so much attention, another variation on that Victorian restraint, may have rendered him even more charming.

Lee Today

When people think about the Confederacy today, they are thinking about something that never existed during their lifetime. There's also the old adage that history is written by the victors. If this is true, reading and learning more about the Confederacy can only help give a more well-rounded view of the past.

The war's relative distance from modern times makes it difficult to be objective. It is recent enough that some people alive today have ancestors who were involved, or perhaps even died, in the war. It is distant enough, though, that plenty of rumors and folklore have had time to grow.

In modern times, since Lee is so removed from most people's lives, opinions on him can drift pretty far away from the factual. It's very tempting to believe anecdotes about Lee at face value. Sometimes, anecdotes can conflict, be exaggerated, or both.

One of Lee's aunt's slaves joined him on his first army assignment. The slave, Nat, was much older and suffered from consumption. Based on the information available from Lee's letters, Nat stayed in quarters about fifteen miles away from Lee. His illness got the better of him. Lee didn't know he had died until someone told him. Lee wrote to Mary, "I had not the least idea he was so low … I was perfectly shocked to hear of his death."

This story has grown into something entirely different in folklore, perhaps because of a letter that Lee's friend wrote about the incident. Lee had made sure that the slave "had the best medical advice, comfortable room, and everything that could be done to restore him." Some versions even say that Lee nursed Nat with "the tenderness of a son," and that when he died, Lee mourned over his grave. None of this is corroborated with Lee's letters. Historian Elizabeth Brown Pryor, who points out this rumor, also notes that the

Many songs exist from the Civil War, including "Sword of General Lee." Lee's sword was for show, as he did not engage in combat.

mother of another friend, Mrs. Eliza Mackay, actually did take care of Nat in his final days. Lee, the young man fresh out of college, did not.

Another conflicting story about Lee's dealing with his slaves began with two letters published in the *New York Tribune* in 1859. The letters accused Lee of cruelty toward two of his slaves at Arlington, Wesley and Mary Norris. Lee hired both Wesley and Mary in the late 1850s. They had belonged to George Custis, Lee's father-in-law. According to the slaves, Custis had told them they would be free upon his death. Lee was instructed to free them within five years by Custis's will. Wesley and Mary escaped in the spring of 1859 with some of their cousins but were captured in Maryland and sent back to Arlington. The letter to the paper writes that they were taken to a barn and whipped. The letter also relates that when the slave-whipper (likely a local sheriff) refused to whip Mary, Lee stepped in and did it himself.

Lee did not respond publicly to the letter. Years later, when the *Baltimore American* reprinted it, he wrote in a letter to the paper: "I have not thought proper to publish a contradiction, being unwilling to be drawn into a newspaper discussion, believing that those who know me would not credit it; and those who do not, would care nothing about it." Lee likely saw his silence on the matter as the dignified approach.

Another account of the event exists, however: Wesley's. He testified to the National Antislavery Standard in 1866 and corroborated that "We were tied firmly to posts by a Mr. Gwin, our overseer, who was ordered by Gen. Lee to strip us to the waist and give us fifty lashes each, excepting my sister, who received but twenty." He does not mention that Lee whipped Mary himself. According to Norris, however, Mr. Gwin couldn't bring himself to do the whipping, so a constable did it. Lee stood by, telling the man to "lay it on well." This is disturbing, but the many versions of the story that exist demonstrate that they cannot all be true. It also has to be noted that the narratives of slaves and free blacks are much scarcer than that of white people, and future historians would do well to include more black voices.

Aside from falling victim to rumors and folklore, the tendency when studying Lee, or any historical figure, is to view him from a modern lens. Inevitably, present-day students and thinkers view Lee with a modernist viewpoint that he did not himself espouse. Should someone who lived in the nineteenth century be judged with a modernist lens? Some historians say no. Carmichael, for instance, points out the difference between knowing what people thought and how people thought. Because our thoughts about the past are so wrapped up in morals, religion, or modern politics, people often become incapable of seeing the past through the eyes of the people who lived through it. In labeling Lee as a villain, or accepting him unconditionally as a hero, how much can really be learned?

Admittedly, it is difficult to be objective for someone whose heritage is being discussed. For people whose ancestors fought in either side of the war, or whose ancestors were slaves, it may be hard to see the other side or even acknowledge that the other side is worth considering.

Those who do want to honor the Confederacy have formed groups, such as the Sons and Daughters of

Confederate Veterans. As their names suggest, people in these groups want to honor their ancestors who fought in the Confederacy. These groups, however, are sometimes accused of being hate groups. A hate group, defined by the Southern Poverty Law Center (SPLC), is "an organization that–based on its official statements or principles, the statements of its leaders, or its activities–has beliefs or practices that attack or malign an entire class of people, typically for their immutable characteristics." Sometimes, hateful racists do join heritage groups looking for compatriots. In recent years, the Sons of Confederate Veterans has attracted lots of extremists, people who seem to want to resurrect the values of the Confederacy. Some of these extremists call themselves Neo-Confederates.

The SPLC estimates that there are 917 chapters of hate groups currently operating in the United States. Neo-Confederate groups are included in this list. While some Neo-Confederates have joined Southern heritage groups, heritage groups should not be confused with hate groups.

No matter one's beliefs on secession or slavery, it is skewed to hold people accountable for their ancestors' beliefs, and worse still to accuse them of being part of a hate group if they are not. Doing so is an example of what Carmichael might call the "victimization mentality." Instead of engaging each other in actual dialogue, people hurl accusations. Carmichael writes, "We are trapped in an endless cycle of conspiratorial charges and counter-charges." The majority of people looking back at this period of history are not able to be objective, or do not realize how subjective their views are.

Just as some mourners turned Lee into a god or a saint after his death, some continue to do so with the memory of the Confederacy. The Confederacy, much like Lee himself, is a sort of vessel that people today can fill with their opinions, wishes, and perhaps regrets. For instance, many people who have no connection to it, at least not in its original context, fly the Confederate battle flag today. Historical objects and people become co-opted (to put it negatively) or repurposed (to put it positively) by future generations, and this is normal. It is easy to lose sight of the original meaning and context of these artifacts. The initial purpose of the Confederate battle flag was to lead soldiers, specifically those of the Army of Northern Virginia, in battle. It represented what the Confederacy stood for, including the institution of slavery. Today, people use it for all kinds of reasons, often directed at the current political climate. Like the original Confederates, some people fly the Confederate flag because they are discontented with their government. Some people fly it for the ambiguous reason that it is part of their heritage, even if it isn't. It is crucial to understand the original associations that this item carries.

Twenty-first century headlines have been peppered with stories about Confederate statues and monuments being taken down. At times, these are accompanied by protests and counterprotests. Some who advocate for getting rid of Confederate imagery do so because they associate such imagery directly with racism and slavery. Kevin Thornton writes, "To read the Confederacy solely in terms of slavery is to create a counter-myth to the Lost Cause, and to cast Southern history solely in the satisfying, though inaccurate, terminology of good and evil." Truly, in some people's eyes

Washington and Lee University, where Lee lived the last few years of his life and is buried

today, the Confederacy and Lee's name are synonymous with slavery. They have every right to remind others of the nation's shameful past, yet that is not a holistic view of history. As for Lee himself, he has said that he did not support the presence of Confederate monuments. He wrote in 1869 that the country should "not to keep open the sores of war but to follow the examples of those nations who endeavored to obliterate the marks of civil strife."

People have all kinds of reasons for appreciating Confederate imagery and Confederate icons. Some do so for the reason of remembering the past. It's important to remember the past, but it's crucial to view all sides of it. People should give a voice to minorities that were not heard in the nineteenth century. It is unfortunate that the war that set "brother against brother" continues to divide the nation in some ways. In remembering the past, we would do well to try not to repeat their mistakes.

abolitionism The view that slavery is wrong and should be ended immediately, not gradually.

American Colonization Society An organization that advocated for the relocation of freed slaves to other countries, namely Africa, out of the belief that a) the inequality with whites would be too deep to overcome, and sometimes b) free blacks would encourage current slaves to revolt.

Arlington Now known as Arlington National Cemetery, the plantation and house that Mary Custis Lee's parents owned, then passed down to her and Robert.

Confederate battle flag The flag that displays a blue X-shape with white stars on a red background, which the Army of Northern Virginia flew under Lee in battle.

conscription Drafting citizens into military service. This was not allowed in the original Constitution but was eventually employed by both the Northern and Southern armies.

Democrat Political party that, at the time of James Buchanan, was split on its convictions on slavery.

fort A military station at which duties and taxes are collected by passing vehicles.

Glossary

gradual emancipation An alternative to emancipating a slave immediately: under a gradual emancipation law, a slave would be a slave until a specified date in the future, after which he or she would be freed.

habeas corpus The legal principle that a citizen cannot be held unless proven guilty. A writ of habeas corpus allows a person to report unlawful detention.

Lost Cause The nostalgic term that Southerners had for the Civil War after it was over.

manumission A master individually freeing his slave. Some slave states made this illegal.

popular sovereignty Introduced with Stephen Douglas's Kansas Nebraska Act, it leaves the decision to allow or disallow slavery up to the territories, not the federal government.

Republican Political party that formed in response to the popular sovereignty decision brought about by the Kansas-Nebraska Act.

1807

Robert E. Lee is born on January 19 in Stratford Hall.

1829

Lee graduates second in his class from West Point. He is commissioned in the Corps of Engineers. His first assignment is on Cockspur Island, Georgia.

1831

Lee marries Mary Randolph Custis on June 30. He begins assignment at Fort Monroe.

1846

Mexican War breaks out. Lee is ordered to report to San Antonio de Bexar, Texas.

1848

Mexican War ends. Lee returns home to Arlington.

1852

Lee becomes superintendent at West Point in the fall.

1855

Lee receives new orders to be the Lieutenant Colonel of the Second Cavalry under Albert Sydney Johnston.

1859

Lee is sent to respond to John Brown's raid on Harpers Ferry in October.

1860

South Carolina secedes from the Union on December 20.

1861

Confederacy is organized at Montgomery on February 9. Confederacy fires on Fort Sumter on April 12, the "last straw" in a series of overtakings of federal property. Virginia secedes on April 17. Lee notifies Scott of his resignation from the federal army.

1862

Lee is sent to fill in for the wounded Joseph Eggleston Johnston and his Army of Northern Virginia in May. The failed Maryland campaign culminates in the Battle of Sharpsburg (Antietam) in September.

Books

Adams, Charles. *When in the Course of Human Events: Arguing the Case for Southern Secession*. Lanham, MD: Rowman & Littlefield, 2000.

Blount, Roy Jr. *Robert E. Lee: A Life*. New York: Viking Penguin, 2003.

Boatner, Mark M. III. *The Civil War Dictionary*. New York: Crown, 1988.

Eicher, David J. *Robert E. Lee: A Life Portrait*. Dallas: Taylor Trade Publishing, 1997.

Fellman, Michael. *The Making of Robert E. Lee*. New York: Random House, 2000.

Glatthaar, Joseph T. *Soldiering in the Army of Northern Wert, Jeffry D. *A Glorious Army: Robert E. Lee's Triumph, 1862-1863*. New York: Simon & Schuster, 2011.

Websites

The Civil War

http://www.pbs.org/kenburns/civil-war

This page is dedicated to Ken Burns' nine-part documentary and includes background information and video clips.

Civil War Times

http://www.historynet.com/civil-war-times

This online magazine on the Civil War offers many articles dedicated to narrow topics like specific battles, widows, horses and artillery, and more.

Georgia Civil War Heritage Trails

http://www.civilwarheritagetrails.org/civil-war-music/index.html

You can hear, and read the lyrics to, a selection of Civil War songs, including the Confederate favorites "The Bonnie Blue Flag" and "Dixie Land."

Adams, Charles. *When in the Course of Human Events: Arguing the Case for Southern Secession*. Lanham, MD: Rowman & Littlefield, 2000.

Blount, Roy, Jr. *Robert E. Lee: A Life*. New York: Viking Penguin, 2003.

Boatner, Mark M., III. *The Civil War Dictionary*. New York: Crown, 1988.

Carmichael, Peter S. "Truth is mighty & will eventually prevail: Political Correctness, Neo Confederates, and Robert E. Lee." Southern Cultures no. 3 (2011): 6-27. *Literature Resource Center*, EBSCOhost.

Clark, John G., and Edmund J. Campion. January 2017. "Election of Abraham Lincoln." *Salem Press Encyclopedia Research Starters*, EBSCOhost.

Clark, John G., and Dorothy C. Salem. September 2017. "Northwest Ordinance." *Salem Press Encyclopedia Research Starters*, EBSCOhost.

"The Constitution of the United States: A Transcription." National Archives, accessed October 31, 2017. https:/ www.archives.gov/founding-docs/constitution-transcript.

Davis, David Brion. *The Problem of Slavery in the Age of Revolution, 1770-1823*. Ithaca, NY: Cornell University Press, 1975.

Eicher, David J. *Robert E. Lee: A Life Portrait*. Dallas: Taylor Trade Publishing, 1997.

Fellman, Michael. *The Making of Robert E. Lee*. New York: Random House, 2000.

Fortin, Jacey. "What Robert E. Lee Wrote to the *Times* About Slavery in 1858." *New York Times*, August 18, 2017. https://www.nytimes.com/2017/08/18/us/robert-e-lee-slaves.html?_r=0

"Gen. Robert E. Lee." *New York Times Learning Network*. 2011.

Hall, Aaron A. "Reframing the Fathers' Constitution: The Centralized State and Centrality of Slavery in the Confederate Constitutional Order." *The Journal of Southern History* 83, no. 2, (2017): 255-296.

Horn, Jonathan. *The Man Who Would Not Be Washington: Robert E. Lee's Civil War and His Decision That Changed American History*. New York: Scribner, 2015.

House of Representatives. "Thirty-Fourth Day—Friday, March 28, 1862." *Journal of the Confederate Congress*, 5. (1862): 156-7. Accessed through US Library of Congress.

Kammer, Charles L. January 2016. "Nat Turner." *Salem Press Biographical Encyclopedia*, EBSCOhost.

"Kansas-Nebraska Act." 2017. *Columbia Electronic Encyclopedia, 6th Edition* 1. Academic Search Premier, EBSCOhost.

Loos, John L. and Thomas L. Altherr. January 2017. "Louisiana Purchase." *Salem Press Encyclopedia*, EBSCOhost.

Melish, Joanne Pope. *Disowning Slavery: Gradual Emancipation and "Race" in New England, 1780-1860.* Ithaca, NY: Cornell University Press, 1998.

"Missouri Compromise." 2017. *Columbia Electronic Encyclopedia, 6th Edition*. EBSCOhost.

Myers, Cayce. "Southern Traitor or American Hero? The Representation of Robert E. Lee in the Northern Press from 1865 to 1870." *Journalism History* 41, no. 4 (2016): 211-221.

O'Connor, Thomas H. "Slavery in the North." *In The Meaning of Slavery in the North*, edited by David Roediger and Martin H. Blatt, 45-53. New York: Garland Publishing, 1998.

Plummer, Mark A., and Susan M. Taylor. January 2017. "Establishment of the Confederate States of America." *Salem Press Encyclopedia*, EBSCOhost.

Pryor, Elizabeth Brown. "Robert E. Lee and Slavery: the general's own words plainly state his view of the Peculiar Institution." *Civil War Times* 48, no. 1 (2009): 30-40.

Ruth, Michael. January 2016. "U.S. Confederate Flag." *Salem Press Encyclopedia*, EBSCOhost. *Southern Poverty Law Center*. www.splcenter.org.

Wright, Joshua D. and Victoria M. Esses. "Support for the Confederate Battle Flag in the Southern United States: Racism or Southern Pride?" *Journal of Social and Political Psychology* 5, no. 1 (2017): 224-254. EBSCOhost, doi: 10.5964/jspp.v5i1.687.

Yarema, Allan. "Riveting the Chains of Slavery: The Irony of the American Colonization Society." *Southern Studies: An Interdisciplinary Journal of the South* 16, no. 2 (2009): 50-67.

Zinn, Howard, adapted by Rebecca Stefoff. *A Young People's History of the United States: Columbus to the War on Terror*. New York: Seven Stories Press, 2009.

Page numbers
in **boldface** are illustrations.

abolitionism, 18–19, 29, 76,
78–79, 81
American Colonization
Society, 24–25, 81–82
Arlington (estate), 45–46,
49–50, 75–76, 81–82, 95
Army of Northern Virginia,
5–6, 9, 14–15, 52, 55, 83, 98

Battle of Second Manassas
(Second Battle of Bull
Run), the, 10, 52
Battle of Sharpsburg
(Antietam), 10, 53, 61
Brown, John, 22, 29, **30**, 31,
50

Confederacy, the, 6, 9–10, 15,
33, 35, 38–39, 50–52, 56,
58, 73–75, 83, 89, 92–93,
96–99
Confederate battle flag, 15,
83–85, 98
Confederate Constitution,
the, 34–35, **36**, 38
conscription, 35–36

Davis, Jefferson, 9, 14, 36, 38,
50–52, 56
Democrat, 32, 83

fort, 6, 8–9, 39, 45, 49, 52, 58,
88–89
Fort Sumter, 39, **39**, 88–89

Garrison, William Lloyd,
24–25, 29, 31, 79
Gettysburg, 10, 54–56
gradual emancipation, 18
"Granny Lee," 10, 51–52
Grant, Ulysses, 10, 49, 54, 56,
58–59

habeas corpus, 89

Jackson, Thomas "Stonewall,"
40, 53–54, 60–61

Lee, Anne (mother), 6,
44–45, 65, 68, 75
Lee, Henry "Light Horse
Harry," 6, 17, 42–45, 64–65
Lee, Mary Randolph Custis
(wife), 46–47, **48**, 49–50, 53,
71, 80–82, 93
Lincoln, Abraham, 31–32,
39, 76, 88–89
Lost Cause, 69, 71, 73, 98

manumission, 18

popular sovereignty, 19,
22–23

About the Author

Alison Gaines is a writer from Vancouver, Washington. She has a bachelor's degree from Knox College. Other titles from her include *Mary Edwards Walker: The Only Female Medal of Honor Recipient* and *Invasive Birds and Plants*. She lives in Gainesville, Florida, where she is obtaining a Master of Fine Arts in poetry at the University of Florida.